THE
BEATLES